THE ROMAN EMPIRE

Foundation story

Fiona Reynoldson

Heinemann Educational,
a division of Heinemann Educational Books Ltd,
Halley Court, Jordan Hill, Oxford OX2 8EJ

OXFORD LONDON EDINBURGH MADRID
ATHENS BOLOGNA PARIS MELBOURNE
SYDNEY AUCKLAND SINGAPORE TOKYO
IBADAN NAIROBI HARARE GABORONE
PORTSMOUTH NH (USA)

© Fiona Reynoldson 1994

The moral right of the proprietor has been asserted

First published 1994

British Library Cataloguing in Publication Data available from the British Library on request.

ISBN 0–435–31679–6

Designed by Ron Kamen, Green Door Design Ltd, Basingstoke

Illustrated by Jeff Edwards Douglas Hall Peter Hicks Stuart Hughes Terry Thomas

Produced by Mandarin Offset
Printed in Hong Kong

Front cover shows Hadrian's Villa in Rome and a statue of a Roman consul.

Acknowledgements

The author and publisher would like to thank the following for permission to reproduce photographs:
Ancient Art & Architecture Collection: Cover, 3.3A, 4.2A
Archäologisches Landesmuseum, Schleswig: 4.1A
Archivio Moro, Rome: 4.6A
Ashmolean Museum: 1.1F
Bibliothèque Nationale: 4.3E
The Trustees of the British Museum: 1.2D, 2.1B, 2.2B, 2.4B, 2.5A, 2.9A, 2.9B, 3.12A, D and E, 4.2C, 4.4A
Simon Chapman: 4.6C
Committee for Aerial Photography, Cambridge: p25
C. M. Dixon: Front cover, 1.2E, 2.1C, 2.3A and C, 2.6E, 3.3C, 3.4B, 3.5B and C, 3.7A, C and D, 3.8A, 3.10A, 3.11A and C, 4.1C
Sonia Halliday Photographs: 2.2C, 2.4C, 3.5A, 3.8B, 3.8D (F. H. C. Birch), 4.5A and B
Michael Holford: Cover, 1.1A, 1.1D, 3.5B, 3.9C, 3.11D
Israel Museum, Jerusalem: 1.2C
Lion Publishing plc/David Townsend: 1.2A
Mansell Collection: p25
Alan Millard: 1.1E
Museum of London: 4.4F
The National Gallery: 4.6B
National Museum of Ireland: 4.1D
Nationalmuseet, Copenhagen: 3.2G
Dr P. J. Reynolds/Butser Ancient Farm: 3.9D
Rheinisches Landesmuseum, Trier: 3.5A, 3.10B and C
Chris Ridgers: 4.6D
Römisch-Germanisches Museum: 2.9D
Tyne & Wear Museum Service: 3.1D
Vatican Museum: 2.1A
Roger Wood: 3.8C

Woodmansterne Picture Library/Museum of London: 3.9A
We are also grateful to the following for permission to reproduce copyright material:
Andromeda Oxford Ltd for Source 3.7B, taken from *Atlas of the Roman World* by Tim Cornell and John Matthews, Phaidon Press, 1982; B. T. Batsford Ltd for Source 1.2B, taken from *England Before Domesday* by Martin Jones; Longman Group UK Ltd for Source 1.3A, taken from *The Romans in Britain* by Dorothy Morrison, 1978.

Every effort has been made to contact copyright holders of material reproduced in this book. Any omissions will be rectified in subsequent printings if notice is given to the publisher.

Details of Written Sources

In some sources the wording or sentence structure has been simplified to ensure that the source is accessible.

The Anglo-Saxon Chronicle (Trans. G. N. Garmonsway), J. M. Dent and Sons Ltd, 1953: 4.4C
Saint Augustine, *City of God* (Ed. David Knowles), Penguin, 1972: 4.2B
D. Breeze and B. Dobson, *Hadrian's Wall*, Allen Lane, 1976: 2.6B
Julius Caesar, *Commentaries* (Ed. R. L. A. Du Pontet), Oxford University Press, 1900: 2.7A
Simon Esmonde Cleary, *The Ending of Roman Britain*, Barnes and Noble Books, 1989: 4.4E
Tim Cornell and John Matthews, *Atlas of the Roman World*, Phaidon Press, 1982: 2.1D, 2.2A, 2.5B, 3.2F, 3.4C
K. Greene, *Archaeology of the Roman Economy*, Batsford, 1986: 3.4D
Catherine Hills, *Blood of the British from Ice Age to Norman Conquest*, George Philip in association with Channel 4 TV company, 1986: 4.3D
J. Liversidge, *Roman Britain*, Longman, 1958: 2.8A
A. Millard, *Discoveries from the Time of Jesus*, Lion, 1990: 2.3B, 2.9E, 3.11B, 3.12B and C
R. W. Moore, *The Roman Commonwealth*, English Universities Press, 1942: 3.3D
Oxford Dictionary of Quotations, Oxford University Press, 1982: 1.1C
J. Percival, *The Roman Villa: a Historical Introduction*, Batsford, 1976: 4.1B, 4.3B and C
Michael Postan, *The Medieval Economy and Society*, Weidenfeld and Nicolson, 1972: 4.4G
J. M. Roberts, *History of the World*, Penguin, 1980: 2.6A and C, 4.5C
R. R. Sellman, *Roman Britain*, Methuen, 1956: 2.8B
Diodorus Siculus, *Library of History* (Trans. C. H. Oldfather), Heinemann, 1939: 2.7B
P. Salway, *Roman Britain*, Oxford University Press, 1981: 2.5E, 2.6D, 2.8C, 2.9CL.
A. Thompson, *Romans and Blacks*, Routledge, 1989: 3.2A, B, C and E
G. I. F. Tingay and J. Badcock, *These Were the Romans*, Hulton, 1972: 3.1A
G. M. Trevelyan, *History of England*, Longman, 1926: 4.4D

CONTENTS

PART ONE   PIECES OF THE PAST
1.1 Words from the Past — 4
1.2 Pieces of the Past — 6
1.3 Secondary Sources — 8

PART TWO   BUILDING AN EMPIRE
2.1 Roman Rise to Power — 10
2.2 Rivals for Trade — 12
2.3 The Roman Army — 14
2.4 The Roman Republic — 16
2.5 Building an Empire — 18
2.6 The Rise of the Dictators — 20
2.7 Case Study 1: Caesar Invades Britain — 22
2.8 Case Study 2: Claudius Invades Britain — 24
2.9 The Emperors — 26

PART THREE   LIVING IN THE EMPIRE
3.1 Citizens — 28
3.2 Barbarians — 30
3.3 The Family — 32
3.4 Transport — 34
3.5 Trade in the Empire — 36
3.6 Roman Towns and Cities — 38
3.7 Buildings in Towns and Cities — 40
3.8 Living in Towns and Cities — 42
3.9 Life in the Countryside — 44
3.10 Roman Villas — 46
3.11 Religious Beliefs — 48
3.12 The First Christians — 50

PART FOUR   END OF THE EMPIRE
4.1 The Empire in Crisis — 52
4.2 The Collapse of the Empire — 54
4.3 The Collapse of the Empire: Gaul — 56
4.4 The Collapse of the Empire: Britain — 58
4.5 Survival in the East — 60
4.6 The Importance of Rome — 62
Index — 64

1.1 Words from the Past

Primary sources

Look at Source A. This is a primary source. A primary source is one that comes from the time the historian is studying. Source A is written in Latin. Latin was the main language spoken in the Roman Empire.

Questions to ask about written primary sources:

- When was it written?
- Who wrote it?
- Why did someone write it?
- Who told the writer the information for it?

You may not be able to answer all these questions about every primary source you use.

A A curse written in Latin on a piece of lead. It says: 'He who stole Vilbia from me, may he waste away like water.'

Source C

Source C is different. It is a primary source. But Virgil did not write in English and he did not type his poem on this piece of paper. This is a copy.

Questions to ask about copied sources:

- If it is a copy, is it copied correctly?
- Has it been changed from one language into another?
- Has changing the language changed the sense?

B Many snakes and other kinds of wild beasts live there, and the local people say that if a man crosses Hadrian's Wall he dies, unable to stand the poisoned air.

A Roman, writing about northern Britain in the 6th century AD.

C I saw you picking
Dewy apples with your
    mother...
How I saw you
How I fell in love!

A poem written by Virgil in the 1st century BC.

4 THE ROMAN EMPIRE

D

SOURCE

This carving from Hadrian's Wall is from AD 142. It says: 'A detachment of the 20th Legion of Valeria and Victrix made this'.

E

SOURCE

This writing is in Greek. It says Pekysis paid his taxes on 12 July, AD 144.

F

SOURCE

This writing is in Greek. It dates from the 1st century AD.

Questions

Read **Primary sources**.

1. Write one sentence saying what a primary source is.

2. Copy the table below. Next to each source letter, write the date the source was made. If you don't know, write 'Don't know'.

SOURCE	DATE
A	
B	
C	
D	
E	
F	

Look at all the sources.

3. Which sources would you use to learn about people's feelings at the time?

Look at Source B.

4. How do you know that this Roman never visited northern Britain?

Think About:

What three written sources would best tell an historian a hundred years from now what your school was like?

1.2 Pieces of the Past

A Roman house from the 1st century AD.

Non-written primary sources

Not all primary sources are written down. Some primary sources are objects. All the sources on pages 6 and 7 are primary sources. They were made in Roman times.

Archaeologists

Archaeologists are people who dig into the ground, looking for things from the past. These things can be everyday objects like pots, mirrors, swords, shoes and combs. Archaeologists even look for whole houses. All these things are primary sources.

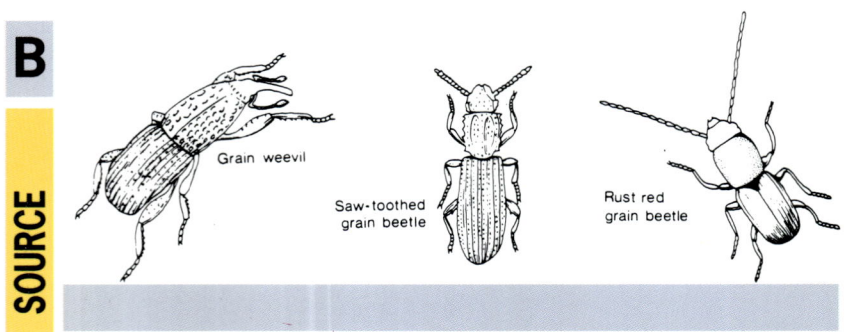

Drawings of insects found by archaeologists in a Roman building.

A sandal from about AD 74.

D SOURCE

A Roman silver bowl, found in England. It was buried in AD 360, to keep it safe from robbers.

E SOURCE

A picture of a woman from Italy. It dates from the 1st century AD.

Questions

Look at all the sources.
1 Copy from the list below all the things that might be non-written primary sources **in Roman times**.

paintings	shoes
microwave ovens	coins
electric kettles	pots
helmets	swords
silver bowls	statues
tombstones	jugs
motor cars	radios

Look at Source A.
2 Describe what you see. What else would you need to know about the house so that you could say what it was like to live in?

1.3 Secondary Sources

Secondary sources
Secondary sources usually come from a time later than the time the historian is studying.

History books
History books, like this one on the Roman Empire, are secondary sources. People who write history books study primary sources and then write down what they have learned about the past. What they write down is a secondary source.

People who write history books do not always agree with each other. They may have used different primary sources. They may look at things differently. You must remember this when you read a history book.

B SOURCE

Primus has made ten tiles.
That is enough.

Scratched on a Roman tile found in London.

C SOURCE

For the last two weeks, Austalis has been wandering off on his own every day.

Scratched on a Roman tile found in London.

An artist's idea of how people in Britain lived before the Romans invaded. It has come from a history book, 'The Romans in Britain', written by Dorothy Morrison in 1978.

A SOURCE

D Sometimes people scratched things onto roof tiles.

From a history book, written in 1993.

E The Romans made roof tiles in London. They were made by slaves who worked very hard. They were watched over all the time by their master.

From a history book, written in 1993.

F A fashionable woman crimps her hair into rows of curls, and builds it up high.

Written by Juvenal, a Roman.

G

A Roman woman, drawn in 1994.

Questions

Read both the paragraphs on page 8.
1 What is a secondary source?

Read Sources B and C.
Then read Sources D and E.
2 Copy the sentences below. Choose one of the words in *italics* each time there is a choice.
Sources B and C are *primary/secondary* sources. This is because the tiles date from *modern/Roman* times. Sources D and E are *primary/secondary* sources. This is because they are written in *Roman/modern* times.

Read Sources B and C. Imagine that this is all you have ever read or seen about Roman tiles.
3 a Read Source D. Is it true or false?
b Read Source E. Is it true or false?

Read Source F and look at Source G.
4 The artist has read Source F. Then he has drawn the picture.
Has he drawn Source G **exactly** as a Roman woman's hair is described in Source F?

> **Think about:**
> What information would you need to draw a Roman tile exactly as it would have looked in Roman times?

THE ROMAN EMPIRE

2.1 Roman Rise to Power

Romulus
The city of Rome began in about 750 BC. There is a legend that it was started by a man called Romulus.

The Etruscans
The Etruscans came from Etruria, near Rome. From about 600 BC the Etruscans ruled Rome. They were good at making things from metal. They made everything from swords to mirrors of polished metal. They were good at building. They built drains and houses.

The Roman Republic from 510 BC
In about 510 BC, the Romans threw out the Etruscan king. Rome became a republic. This is a place ruled without a king or queen.

Rome gets stronger
Slowly the Romans conquered more and more land in Italy. The Romans fought off the Greeks and the Gauls (see the map on this page). By 265 BC Rome controlled Italy. About three million people lived in Italy then.

Roads, armies and Latin
The Romans built good roads. They had a strong army. They made sure the places they conquered were well ruled. More and more Italians accepted Roman rule. They spoke Latin.

A SOURCE

A mirror made by an Etruscan.

Early Rome and its neighbours.

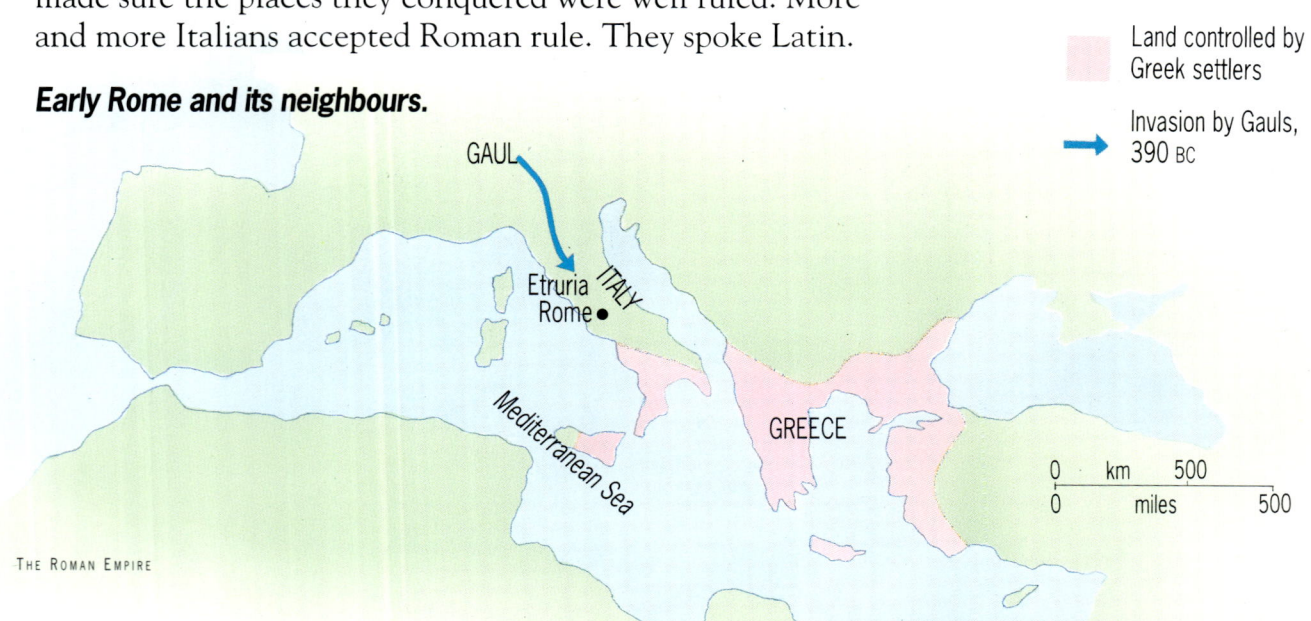

B SOURCE

A Roman coin made in the 1st century BC. It celebrates a Roman victory.

D SOURCE

Have you ever seen a more richly farmed land than Italy?

Written by Varro, a Roman who lived in the 1st century BC.

C SOURCE

How Rome got its name.

The legend says that Romulus and Remus were the twin grandsons of a king. When he died, they were left by a river to die, to stop them ruling. They were found and raised by a she-wolf. When they grew up they decided to build a great city on the spot where they had been left to die. But they had a row. Romulus killed Remus, and named the city after himself.

Questions

Look at Source C. Read the caption.
1 Draw a comic strip to tell the story of Romulus and Remus. Below are the titles for the pictures:

Romulus and Remus are put by the river to die.
They are looked after by a she-wolf.
They decide to build a city.
Romulus kills Remus.
Romulus calls the city Rome.

Read **The Etruscans**.
2 Write down one thing the Etruscans were good at.

Read **The Roman Republic from 510 BC**.
3 What is a republic?

Look at the sources.
4 Which sources tell you that Rome was doing well by the 1st century BC?

2.2 Rivals for Trade

Trade

Trade is buying and selling things. The people who buy and sell things are called traders.

Roman traders

Traders can make lots of money. For instance, a Roman trader filled his ship full of jars of wine. He sailed to Sicily. He sold the wine for more than he paid for it. He made lots of money. Other traders bought and sold other things.

Traders from Carthage and Greece

However, Romans were not the only traders. There were traders in Greece and Carthage. They wanted to sell wine to people in Sicily or horses to people in Spain. Rome and Carthage started to fight over who traded where.

Hannibal

Hannibal led the Carthaginians against the Romans. He had an army of about 35,000 men and 40 elephants. He set off for Italy. Whenever he reached a big river, he floated the elephants across on rafts. In winter, in the snow and ice, Hannibal crossed the mountains into Italy.

The Romans were taken by surprise. Hannibal won battle after battle for several years. But he could never take Rome itself. In the end the Romans attacked Carthage. Hannibal fled. In 182 BC he took the poison he always carried in a ring on his finger, and died. In 146 BC, the Romans destroyed Carthage and built a new Roman city with the same name.

  The Carthaginians will not harm any Roman subjects.

 The Carthaginians will not build any forts in Roman lands.

From a treaty between Rome and Carthage, made in 201 BC.

Questions

Read **Trade**.
1 Copy the sentences below. Fill in the gaps.
  Trade is buying and _____ things. The people who buy and sell things are called _____.

Read **Roman traders** and **Traders from Carthage and Greece**.
2 Look at the list below. Why did Rome and Carthage go to war? Copy the reason you think is most likely.

  To conquer the world.
  They didn't like each other.
  They argued over where each of them should trade.
  To show they were clever.

Read **Hannibal**.
3 Put the sentences below in **chronological** order. That is the order they happened.
  a Hannibal could never take Rome.
  b He killed himself in 182 BC.
  c Hannibal led an army of 35,000 men and 40 elephants.
  d In 146 BC the Romans destroyed Carthage.
  e Hannibal took the Romans by surprise.
  f He won battle after battle.

SOURCE B: A Roman coin from 125 BC. It celebrates a Roman victory over Carthage in 251 BC.

SOURCE C: The remains of the Roman city of Carthage.

Trade routes at the time of the wars with Carthage.

Trade routes between Greek cities
Trade routes between Carthaginian cities

2.3 The Roman Army

The army got bigger
The Romans had a very good army. At first it was small. But the Roman Empire grew bigger. So they needed a bigger and bigger army to conquer new lands.

Reorganizing the army
By 100 BC the Roman army was reorganized. Many men became full-time soldiers.

How the army was organized

8 men	= 1 contubernium (tent)
10 contubernia	= 1 century (80 men)
6 centuries	= 1 cohort (480 men)
10 cohorts	= 1 legion

A legion was really about 5,400 men. The 1st cohort had 600 extra men. These men worked for the whole army. Some of them were blacksmiths, cooks, messengers, clerks.

B SOURCE

The Emperor Septimus Severus was the first to give them more money and permission to wear gold rings and to live with their wives. This was in AD 197.

Written by Herodian. Before this time soldiers under the rank of centurion were not allowed to marry.

A SOURCE

Roman soldiers building a fort. This picture is of a memorial to the Emperor Trajan. It is called Trajan's column.

Soldiers also built roads and bridges.

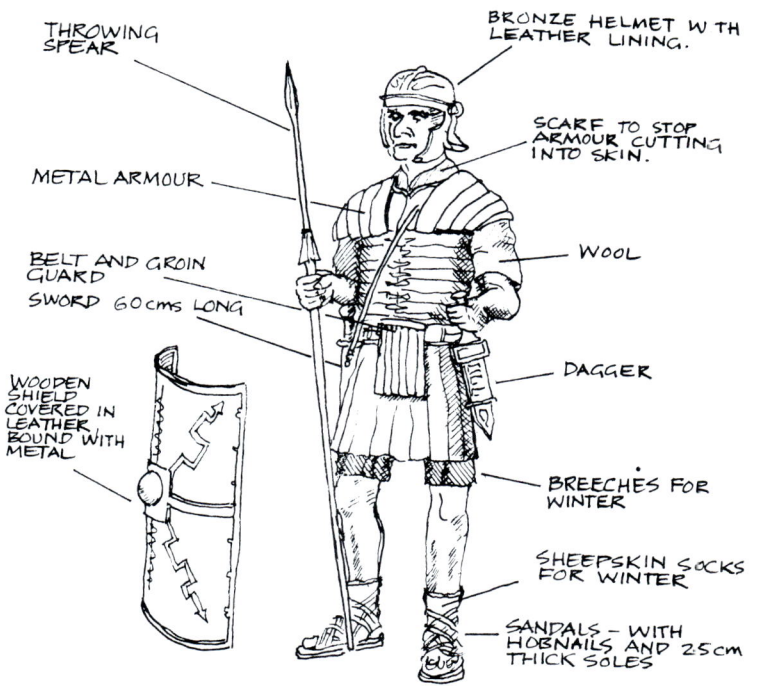

A Roman Legionary.

A Roman carving showing a Roman emperor talking to his soldiers.

> **D** They make a desert and call it 'peace'.

Written by Tacitus, a Roman, in about AD 90. He is describing how the Roman army treated the lands they conquered.

Questions

Read **How the army was organized**.
1. **a** How many men were in a legion?
   b How many men were in a contubernium?

2. The soldiers had to carry everything with them. What do you think they would have needed from the list below?
   kitchen sinks
   armchairs
   spades
   poles to make camp fences
   tents of goat or calf skin
   swords
   wine
   food

Look at the drawing of a Roman Legionary on this page.
3. What else did a Roman soldier carry?

2.4 The Roman Republic

Two consuls were chosen to run the Senate and the army. If Rome was in danger they would appoint a dictator.

The Senate

The Romans made themselves into a republic in 509 BC. They did not have a king any more. Rome was run by the Senate. The men in the Senate made the laws. At first the Senate had 100 members. Later there were many more. Some of the Senators had jobs such as being judges, paying the army or governing parts of the empire.

Citizens

Roman citizens could vote for who they wanted in the Senate. Some citizens were rich. They became senators and made the laws. Sometimes the poor citizens became angry. They wanted to make laws.

Writing the laws down

In 450 BC the poor citizens insisted that Roman laws were written down. Then everyone knew what was fair.

Slowly the poor citizens won the right to have a say in making the laws. But even so the real power lay with the rich citizens.

A The letters SPQR stand for 'Senate and People of Rome'. These letters were put on buildings and army standards.

B A Roman coin made in AD 23. The letters mean 'made by permission of the Senate.'

16 THE ROMAN EMPIRE

Questions

Read **The Senate** and **Citizens**.

1 Copy the following sentences, matching the Heads and Tails.

Rome became	angry.
Rome was run by	laws.
The Senate made	judges.
Some senators were	the Senate.
Rich citizens were most likely	to make laws too.
Poor citizens became	to join the Senate.
Poor citizens wanted	a republic.

Look at all the sources.

2 What evidence is there that the Senate was powerful?

Think about:
Look at Source C.
If this was the town centre what sort of buildings would be around the square?

C The ruins of the Forum in Rome. The Romans built a forum in every Roman town. It was the town centre, with an open space for meetings.

2.5 Building an Empire

An empire
A country has an empire when it conquers lots of other countries and takes control of them. All of the countries it controls are part of its empire.

The Roman Empire and the army
The Romans conquered more and more countries. More and more men joined the Roman army. Soon the Roman army was the biggest and best in the world. With a big army, the Romans could conquer more countries. This is how the Roman Empire grew.

The Roman Empire and trade
Many Romans made a lot of money trading all over the empire. Having an empire meant money and power for the Romans.

More lands conquered
Look at the map on the opposite page. By 30 BC all the land coloured blue had been conquered by Rome. This was a lot of land. But the Roman Empire was still growing. However, by AD 117 the Roman Empire was just about as big as it would ever be.

B SOURCE

I have given them an Empire without limits.

Said by a Roman god in a play written in the 1st century BC.

C SOURCE

The gods desire that Rome shall be the capital of all the world.

Written by Livy, a Roman playwright, in 1st century BC.

D SOURCE

Don't forget, Romans, it is your special skill to rule all peoples.

Written by Virgil, a Roman, in 1st century BC.

E SOURCE

The Romans felt that they had absolute right on their side.

From 'Roman Britain', by P. Salway, 1981.

A SOURCE

A Roman coin which shows the Greek god, Apollo.

Land controlled by Rome by AD 117.

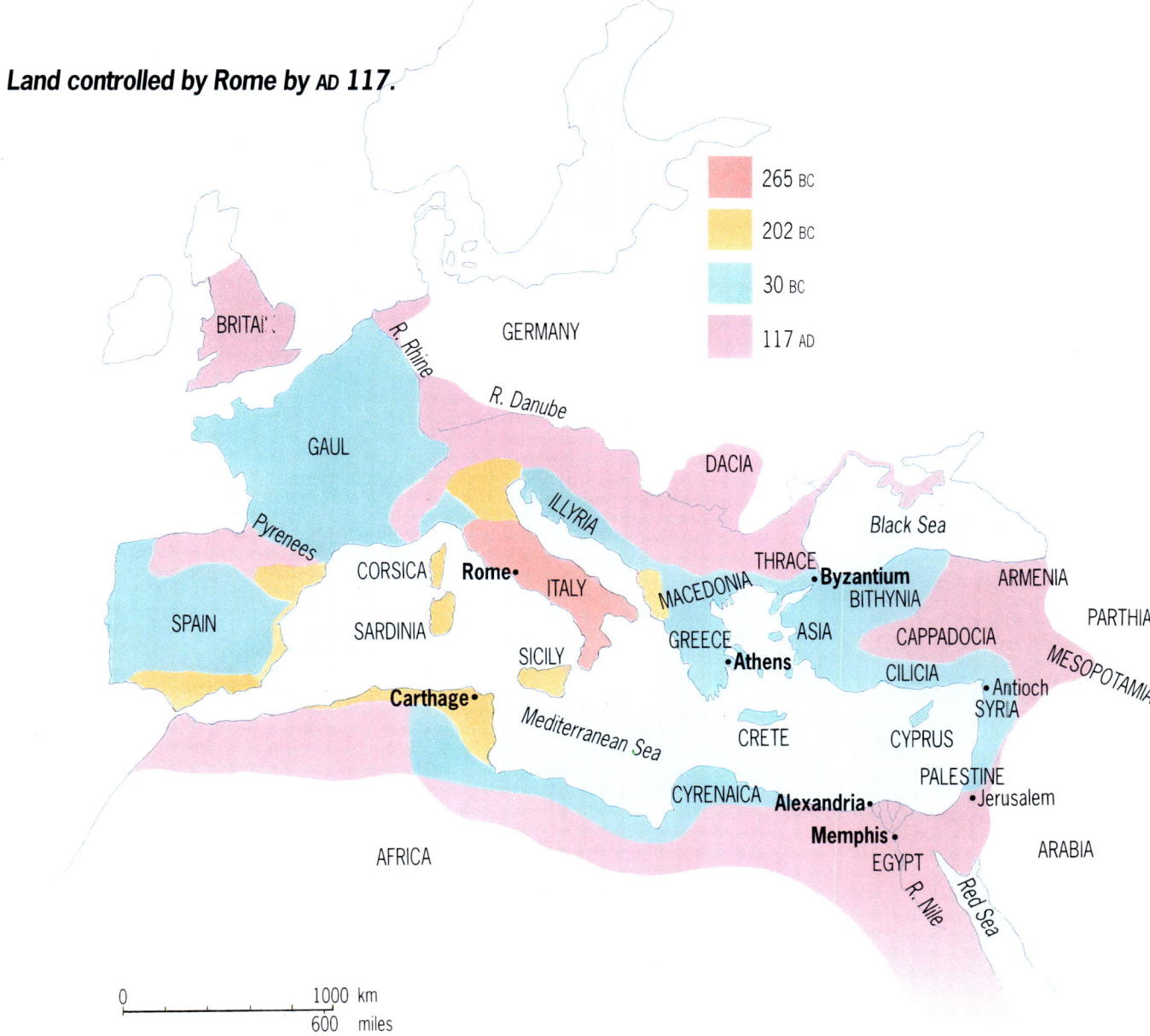

Questions

Read **An empire**.
1 Write a sentence to explain what an empire is.

Look at Source A and the map on this page.
2 When do you think this coin was made?

Look at the map on this page.
3 a Which country did Rome control in 265 BC?
   b Write down all the countries Rome had added to the empire by 30 BC.
   c Write down the countries Rome had added to the empire between 30 BC and AD 117.

2.6 The Rise of the Dictators

Arguments
In the 2nd century BC, rich and poor citizens started to argue about who ran the Roman republic.

Marius and Sulla
Marius was a good general. He made the Roman army bigger and better and became very powerful in Rome. But other army leaders became powerful too. One of these was Sulla. Marius and Sulla fought until Marius died.

Pompey
The next powerful general was Pompey. He made an alliance with two other men. One was a senator called Crassus. The other was a young man called Julius Caesar.

Julius Caesar
Caesar spent ten years leading the army. He conquered the whole of Gaul. His soldiers loved him. They would follow him anywhere. Caesar decided to head back to Rome in 49 BC. He defeated Pompey and seized power for himself.

The plot against Caesar
Julius Caesar was so powerful that many of the senators were afraid of him. A group of senators got together and plotted against Caesar.

Murder – 15 March 44 BC
The senators stabbed Caesar to death in the Senate.

A SOURCE: Caesar was captured by some pirates. He was playing dice with them. He joked that he would crucify them when he was free. He did.

From 'History of the World', by J.M. Roberts, 1980.

B SOURCE: If an ordinary man could ride 50 miles a day, Caesar could ride 100 miles a day.

From 'The Great Commanders', Channel 4 TV, 1993.

C SOURCE: Caesar defeated seven legions in Spain, treated them mildly and won their obedience.

From 'History of the World', by J.M. Roberts, 1980.

D SOURCE: Caesar was a great commander because he was absolutely determined to win.

From 'The Great Commanders', Channel 4 TV, 1993.

Some of Julius Caesar's actions.

Gave land to poor citizens.
Reformed the laws.
Ruled like a king.
Built many fine buildings.
Put his friends in powerful positions.
Named a month after himself (July).
Wore purple robes, like a king.
Introduced a new calendar.
Helped many people in Spain and Gaul to become citizens.
Put up his own statue among the statues of the old kings of Rome.

Questions

Read **Marius and Sulla**.
1 Copy the sentences below. Fill in the gaps.
Marius was a good _____. He made the _____ army bigger and better. Other army _____ became powerful too. One of these was _____.

| Roman | Sulla |
| general | leaders |

Read Caesar's actions in the green box on this page.
2 Write down two headings: **Popular** and **Unpopular**. Copy the things you think would be popular or unpopular under the right heading.

Read Sources B and D.
3 What sort of words best describe Caesar?
Choose from the list below:
lazy   determined   active
busy   relaxed   clever

Think about:
Why was Caesar ruthless some of the time (as in Source A) and sometimes not (as in Source C)?

E A bust (head and shoulders sculpture) of Julius Caesar.

2.7 Case Study 1: Caesar Invades Britain

Why did Caesar invade Britain?

Caesar was a powerful, clever general. He had won many battles in Gaul. The British had been helping the Gauls fight Caesar. This made him angry. He wanted to frighten the British. He was also curious about this wild, cold, damp land. Some people said it was full of rich jewels. Some people said the air was poisonous. Some said strange monsters lurked around the coast. Caesar did not believe all the strange stories he heard. Conquering Britain would add to his fame. So he made plans.

55 BC

It was 55 BC. Caesar set out. He had a small army. When his ships reached Britain, the British were waiting for him. Caesar's soldiers were not keen to leave the ships and wade ashore. The British looked fierce. Then the standard bearer of the Tenth Legion leapt ashore. It was a terrible thing to be a coward in the Roman army, so the others followed. They fought their way ashore and camped. A few days later a storm wrecked many of their ships. They had to repair the ships and make their way back to Gaul.

54 BC

It was 54 BC. Caesar had learnt a bit about Britain. He came back with a larger army. They landed and marched through Kent. They fought several battles. Some of the British were impressed. They decided to go over to the Roman side. In the end Caesar took some hostages. He demanded some money to be paid to Rome each year. Then he went back to Gaul.

Was invading Britain a good idea?

The Romans disagreed about whether it was worth invading Britain. Britain was a wild, faraway country. It was very difficult to get there. No one knew much about it. The sources on pages 22 and 23 give you some different views about Britain.

SOURCE A
There are many men, buildings and herds of animals. There is much wood. The money is bronze or gold.

Written by Julius Caesar, after he had been to Britain. Caesar lived from 100–44 BC.

SOURCE B
Their way of life is simple. There are many people there. Much tin is taken from Britain to Gaul.

Written by Diodorus Siculus, a Roman, in about 30 BC.

SOURCE C
Britain has gold, silver, other metals and pearls.

Written by Tacitus, a Roman, who lived from AD 56–115.

D Caesar hurt the enemy more than he got rich. You could not take anything from people who were so poor.

Written by Plutarch, a Roman, who lived from AD 50–125.

E Caesar defeated the British. He took a lot of money from them.

Written by Suetonius, a Roman, in about AD 120.

F The British do not use money. They get what they want by swapping.

Written by Solinus, a Roman, in about AD 200.

G Some people think that the Britons are named from the word 'brutes', because they are so cut off from the world.

Written by Isidorus Hispalensis, a Roman, in about AD 620.

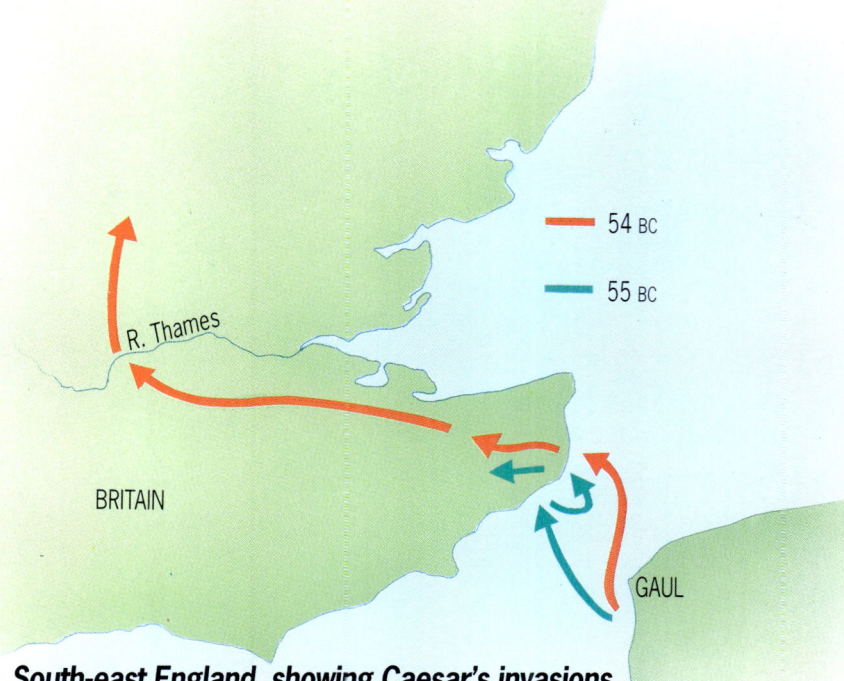
South-east England, showing Caesar's invasions.

Questions

Read **Why did Caesar invade Britain?**

1 Copy the sentences below. Fill in the gaps.
Caesar was a powerful, clever _____. He had won many battles in _____. He knew the _____ were helping the Gauls. Caesar wanted to _____ the British. He was also _____. What sort of a land was _____? The last reason why he wanted to invade Britain was that he wanted to become even more _____.

> British   curious   Britain   Gaul
> frighten   general   famous

Read **55 BC**.

2 Copy the sentences below in **chronological** order. That is the order they happened.
a They made their way back to Gaul.
b The soldiers fought their way ashore.
c Caesar's ships reached Britain.
d The standard bearer of the Tenth Legion leapt ashore.
e The soldiers were afraid.
f A storm wrecked Caesar's ships.

2.8 Case Study 2: Claudius Invades Britain

AD 43

The Emperor Claudius decided to invade Britain. He wanted to show that he was strong. But he had to have an excuse. So Claudius said that a British leader who was friendly to the Romans had been driven out of his lands. Claudius offered to help.

What happened?

The Roman army sailed to Britain and landed in Kent. There was a big battle at the River Medway and the British were thrown back. Now that it looked as if the Romans would win, Claudius came to Britain himself. He only stayed for sixteen days. But his army captured Colchester and defeated the British in the south east of Britain. Satisfied, Claudius went home to Rome.

The conquest continues

The Ninth and Fourteenth Legions marched north and west. The Second Legion continued to march along the south coast. It captured British forts one after another.

How do we know what happened?

It is not easy to find out exactly what happened. On pages 24 and 25 you will read several primary sources that do not agree with each other. You will also read some secondary sources that do not agree with each other.

A SOURCE

Claudius invaded our island. Some Britons welcomed the Romans, others fought them. Bit by bit the Romans conquered all of what we now call England and Wales.

From 'Roman Britain', by J. Liversedge, 1958.

B SOURCE

The Britons made a big effort to defend the River Medway. They were only driven off after a fierce, two-day battle.

From 'Roman Britain', by R. Selman, 1956.

C SOURCE

Claudius received the surrender of eleven British kings, defeated without casualties.

From a Roman carving, 1st century AD.

D SOURCE

Claudius took the triumph without any effort of his own.

Written by the Jewish historian, Josephus, in the 1st century AD.

E Claudius crossed to Britain and joined the Roman army. He took over command, defeated the British and conquered Colchester.

SOURCE

Written by Cassio Dio, a Roman historian, who lived from AD 160–230.

F Vespasian defeated two powerful tribes, partly under the leadership of Aulus Plautus, partly of Claudius. Claudius fought no battles.

SOURCE

Written by Suetonius Tranquillus, in about AD 120.

Maiden Castle, Dorset. A Roman force attacked the British here.

Questions

Read **AD 43**.

1 Copy the sentences below. Fill in the gaps.
The Emperor _____ decided to invade Britain. He needed an excuse. Claudius said that a _____ leader, who was friendly to the _____ had been driven out of his lands. Claudius offered to _____.

> British   Claudius
> Romans   help

Look at all the sources.

2 a List the sources that are primary sources.
  b How can you tell?

Look at Source C.

3 This is an official Roman piece of writing. Do you think it can be trusted? Explain your answer.

> **Think about:**
> Archaeologists found Roman and British weapons at Maiden Castle. They found British cooking pots. Why didn't they find any Roman cooking pots?

THE ROMAN EMPIRE

2.9 The Emperors

The Roman Republic

From 509–27 BC, Rome was a republic. There were no kings or emperors. The last years of the Roman republic were full of civil wars.

SOURCE B

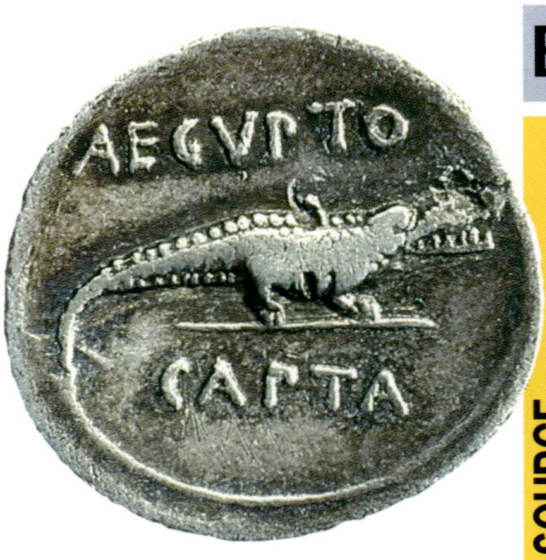

A silver coin made in 28 BC. It marks Augustus adding Egypt to the Roman Empire.

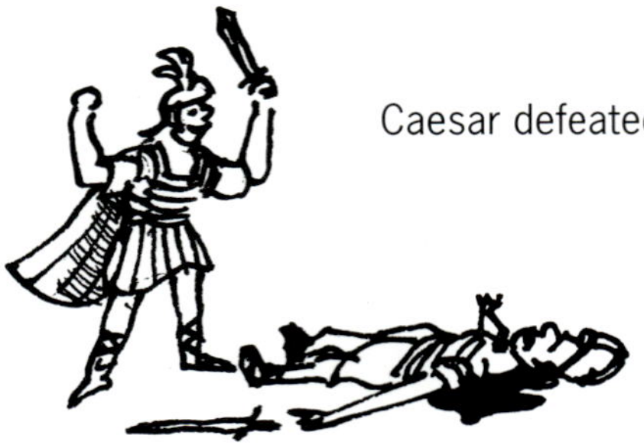

Caesar defeated Pompey.

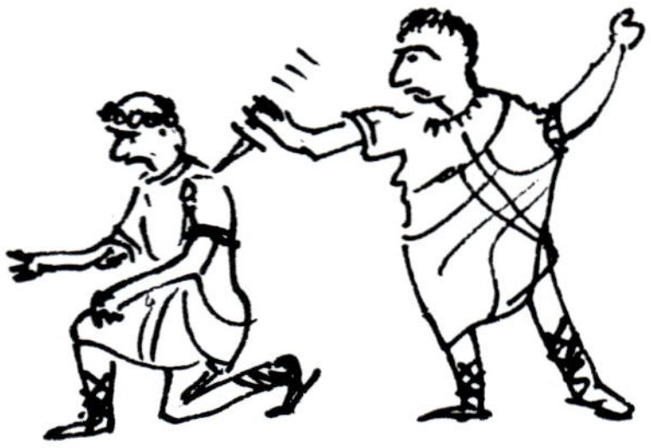

Caesar murdered.

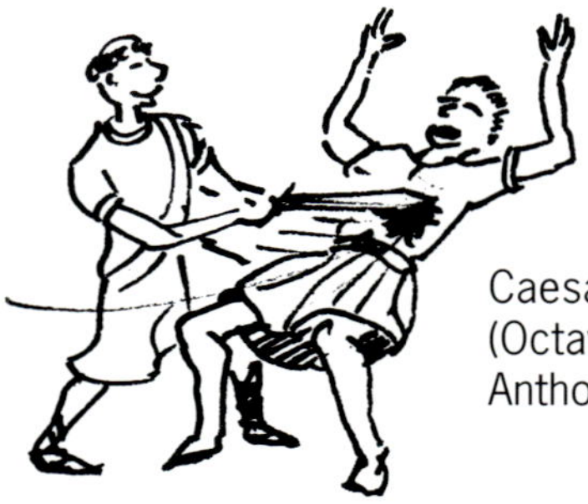

Caesar's nephew (Octavian) defeated Anthony.

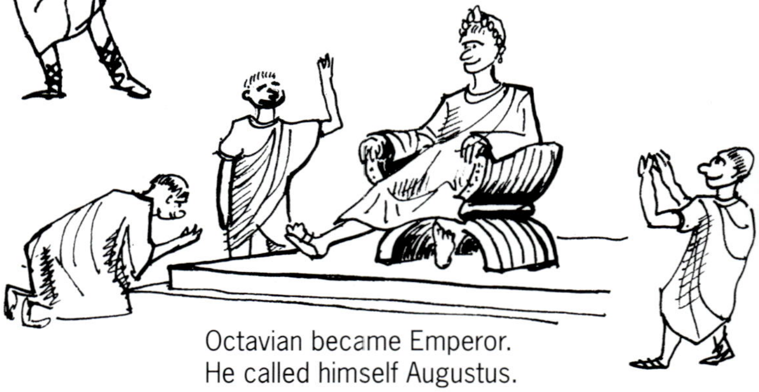

Octavian became Emperor. He called himself Augustus.

SOURCE A

A gold coin. It marks Augustus adding Armenia to the Roman Empire.

SOURCE C

The army was loyal to the emperor's family, not to the Roman Senate or people.

From 'Roman Britain', by P. Selway, 1981.

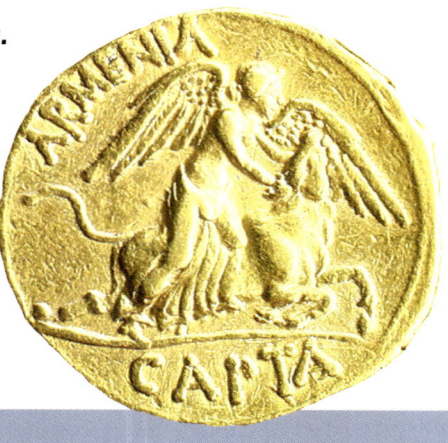

SOURCE D

A head of the Emperor Augustus. Although it was made soon after his death in AD 14, he is made to look like a young man.

The Roman Empire

The civil wars lasted until a strong man took control. This man was Julius Caesar's nephew, Octavian. He said he was going to rule by himself. In 27 BC, he changed his name to Augustus and became the first Roman Emperor. So the years before 27 BC are called 'The Republic', and the years after are called 'The Empire'.

SOURCE E

Augustus improved life for everyone in the Empire.

Augustus was well known for his courage and fairness. This may be because most of his enemies did not live to say otherwise.

From 'Discoveries From the Time of Jesus', by A. Millard, 1980.

Questions

Read **The Roman Republic**.
1 Write down the dates of the Roman Republic.

Below is a list of some famous Roman emperors.
2 Copy the emperors below in **chronological** order. That is the order they ruled.
a Claudius   AD 41–54
b Augustus   27 BC–AD 14
c Hadrian   AD 117–138
d Nero   AD 54–68
e Constantine   AD 312–337
f Caligula   AD 37–41

Look at the sources.
3 'Augustus conquered many countries.'
Which sources support this statement?

Think about:
What differences would there be between Rome when it was ruled by the Republic and when it was ruled by an emperor?

3.1 Citizens

Citizens and their rights and duties

A citizen is a member of a country. A citizen has rights and duties. Citizens rights are what the laws of their country say they can do. Citizens duties are what people have to do to help their country.

Roman citizens

A Roman citizen could join the army, vote in elections and be protected by the law. A Roman citizen had to pay taxes and obey the law. There were three sorts of citizens:

Patricians They were rich. They owned farms and houses. They were often senators and made the laws.

Equites Equites were businessmen. They had less power than patricians.

Plebeians Plebeians were poor. They had very little power.

Sometimes the plebeians demanded to make the laws as well. Sometimes they went on strike or refused to fight in the army. In 450 BC the plebeians insisted the Roman laws were written down so everyone knew what they were. In 492 BC some plebeians became tribunes and were allowed to speak in the Senate.

SOURCE B Paul and Silas were whipped and put in jail. When the soldiers found out Paul and Silas were Roman citizens, they were afraid.

From 'The Bible'.

SOURCE C What use are laws when money calls all the tunes?

Written by Petronius in the 1st century AD.

SOURCE A The most important split in Roman society was between the particians and the plebeians. Only patricians entered the Senate, ran the country, controlled religions. In Rome any marriage between a patrician and a plebeian was forbidden by law.

From 'These Were the Romans', by G.I.F. Tingay and J. Badcock, 1972.

Non-citizens

At first only Romans were citizens. But gradually, some free men were allowed to become Roman citizens. Women and slaves were never citizens.

Slaves

At first there were not many slaves. But as the Romans conquered more countries they took more prisoners. Many prisoners were sold as slaves. A slave had no rights. They were bought and sold like horses or pieces of furniture.

Slaves did many different jobs. Greek slaves were teachers and accountants. Other slaves worked on farms, in homes or in the mines. Some were well treated. Others were beaten or killed. The emperors Augustus and Hadrian passed laws to stop the worst treatment of slaves.

D

The tombstone of a woman called Regina. She was a British slave who was bought by a Roman soldier. He freed her and married her.

Questions

Read **Citizens and their rights and duties**.

1. Write two sentences saying what a citizen is.

2. **a** How many rights did a Roman citizen have?
   b Write down one of the rights that a Roman citizen had.
   c Write down one of the duties that a Roman citizen had.
   d How many sorts of citizens were there?

Look at all the sources.

3. **a** Which source tells you that it was a good thing to be a Roman citizen?
   b 'Slaves had dreadful lives.' How do you know this was not always true?

3.2 Barbarians

Roman views on barbarians
The Romans did not think much of anyone who lived outside the Roman Empire. They called them barbarians.

All sorts of barbarians
There were all sorts of barbarians. They were different tribes of people. The barbarians liked the look of all the things the Romans had. They liked the farms and stone built houses. They liked the towns and theatres. They liked the coins, the jewels, clothes and good food the Romans had. Often the barbarians raided the Roman Empire. The Roman army pushed them back. But when the Roman Empire got weaker the barbarians raided more and more often. In the end many barbarians settled inside the Roman Empire and some even captured Rome.

The sources on pages 30 and 31 show you some of the views the Romans had about barbarians.

A SOURCE
Too tall. Lank blonde or red hair. Light blue eyes. Upturned noses. Huge bellies. Simple minds. Quick tempers. Brave. Reckless. Drunken. Lazy. Gambling and boastful.

Various Roman descriptions of barbarians, from 'Romans and Blacks', by L.A. Thompson, 1989.

B SOURCE
Pale brown faces. Straight nose. Bright brown eyes. Brown hair. Thin lips. Not too tall.

What a Roman should look like, from 'Romans and Blacks', by L.A. Thompson, 1989.

C SOURCE
We change our hair colour to blonde because men find it more attractive.

Written about Roman women copying barbarian ways in the 1st century AD.

D SOURCE
Africans have whiter souls than the whitest of Greeks.

Written by a Roman in about AD 250.

30 THE ROMAN EMPIRE

SOURCE E

The kingdom of Ethiopia is a rich wonderland. It has much gold and a royal family descended from the gods.

Written in a Roman geography book in about AD 250.

SOURCE F

Sulpicius Galga killed thousands of Lusitanians after they surrendered. He was let off at his trial. Few people cared what happened to barbarians.

From 'Atlas of the Roman World', by T. Cornell and J. Matthews, 1982. Lusitanians came from what is now Portugal.

SOURCE G

Roman gold and silver coins from Ginderup in Denmark. They were probably buried there in 100 AD. Archaeologists think they belonged to a barbarian who was in the Roman army. He brought his money home.

Questions

Read **Roman views on barbarians**.

1 Copy the sentences below. Fill in the gaps.
The _____ did not think much of anyone who lived outside the Roman _____.

Empire   Romans

Read **All sorts of barbarians**.

2 Look at the list below. Which sorts of Roman things did the barbarians like?

flowers   jewels   books
farms   clothes   cooking pots
televisions   good food

Read Source A.
3 Draw an identikit face and colour it.

Read Source B.
4 Draw an identikit face and colour it.

Read Source E.
5 Do you trust Source E? Explain your answer.

Think about:
Which sources show that Romans approved of some barbarians? Which sources show that Romans disliked other barbarians?

3.3 The Family

Paterfamilias and materfamilias

The father was the head of the family. He was called paterfamilias. Everyone in the house had to do as he said. His sons had to obey him even after they left home.

Women ran the house. The mother was known as materfamilias.

Women, marriage and childbirth

Women obeyed their fathers. When they married they obeyed their husbands. Parents chose who their children married. Girls could marry at 12 years of age. Most did not marry until they were 14. The night before the wedding, a girl put her toys on the household shrine for the gods. At the wedding a contract was signed and there was a party. Many women died having children. Many small children died young.

Property

In the Roman republic all of a woman's money could go to her husband's father. Later, women controlled their own belongings and had more freedom. Many Roman writers did not like this. They thought women should just run the home. Roman writers were generally men.

B SOURCE

All men rule over women. We Romans rule all men and our wives rule us!

Written by Cato, a Roman writer, who lived from 234–149 BC.

A SOURCE

Statues of a family from Palmira (in modern Syria). These people lived in the Roman Empire. But they would not have lived like a Roman family. They dressed and lived like a middle eastern family.

C A Roman carving of a baby being bathed.

Questions

Read **Paterfamilias and materfamilias** and **Women, marriage and childbirth**.

1 Copy the sentences below, matching the Heads and Tails.

Paterfamilias was	at 12 years of age.
Women were	how the house was run.
Girls could marry	the mother.
Parents chose	controlled by their fathers or husbands.
Materfamilias was	the head of the family.
Women did control	who their children married.

Look at all the sources.
2 Which one tells you that not all people in the Roman Empire lived and dressed in the Roman way?

Read Source D.
3 Choose from the words below the ones you think best describe a good Roman wife.

    busy   independent   faithful   obedient   bossy
        kind   clever   happy   rich   good

D You were a faithful and obedient wife to me. You were kind and friendly. You worked hard at your spinning. You didn't show off your running of the house. You looked after my mother.

Written by a Roman about his wife in the 1st century BC.

3.4 Transport

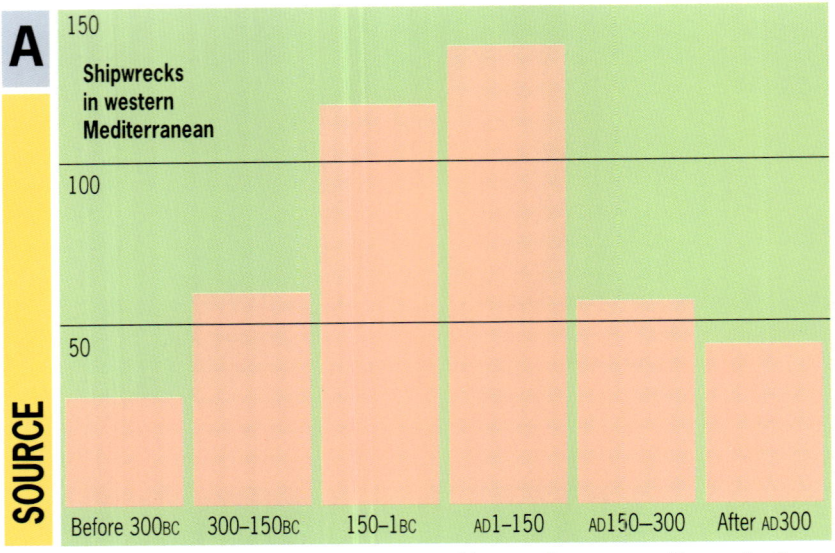

A Shipwrecks in western Mediterranean

How many ancient ships were found by underwater divers in the western Mediterranean.

C Across the lake there is marble, food and timber. It is hard to get it by cart from the lake to the sea. It would take a lot of workmen to join the lake to the sea, but there are plenty here.

From a letter written by Pliny to the Emperor Trajan in about AD 112.

Types of transport

The two main types of transport were by road or ship. Transport was very important to the Romans.

A painting of a Roman ship.

34 THE ROMAN EMPIRE

D SOURCE

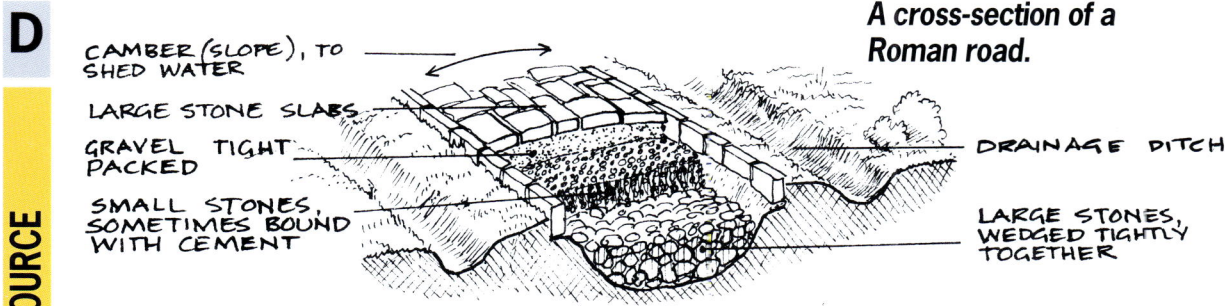

A cross-section of a Roman road.

The importance of transport

Rome had a huge empire. There were three reasons why the Romans needed good roads and lots of ships.
1. The Roman army needed to move about quickly.
2. Carts and ships had to carry food all over the empire.
3. The Romans had to collect taxes (in coins) and carry them back to Rome or to other cities.

How do we know – roads

There are still thousands of miles of Roman roads. We can look at the old Roman roads to see how they were made.

The Romans wrote books about their roads. One of these, the 'Antonine Itinerary', lists 225 routes all over the Roman Empire. It also says how far it is between towns. Roman writings show that people travelled easily from place to place. St. Paul's travels in 'The Bible', could only have happened with good road and sea transport.

How do we know – ships

There are many paintings and mosaics (see Source B) that show ships. Roman books and letters tell us about the grain and wine that was carried in ships from places like North Africa to Italy. Underwater divers have found old Roman ships that have sunk, and these tell us a lot about how the ships were made and what they carried.

The Romans built canals as well and we can still see parts of these in places like Germany and Britain.

Questions

Read **Types of transport** and **The importance of transport**.
1. Copy the sentences below. Choose the one of the words in *italics* each time there is a choice.
   The two main types of transport were by *rail/road* and *ship/shop*. The Romans needed many roads and ships to move the *army/artists* around the empire quickly. They also needed to send *feet/food* around the empire and to collect *taxis/taxes* from people in the empire.

Look at Source C.
2. What is Pliny suggesting the emperor should do?

Look at Source B.
3. a A ship's captain was called 'Magister' in Latin. What is the name of the captain of this ship?
   b What do you think the ship is transporting?

3.5 Trade in the Empire

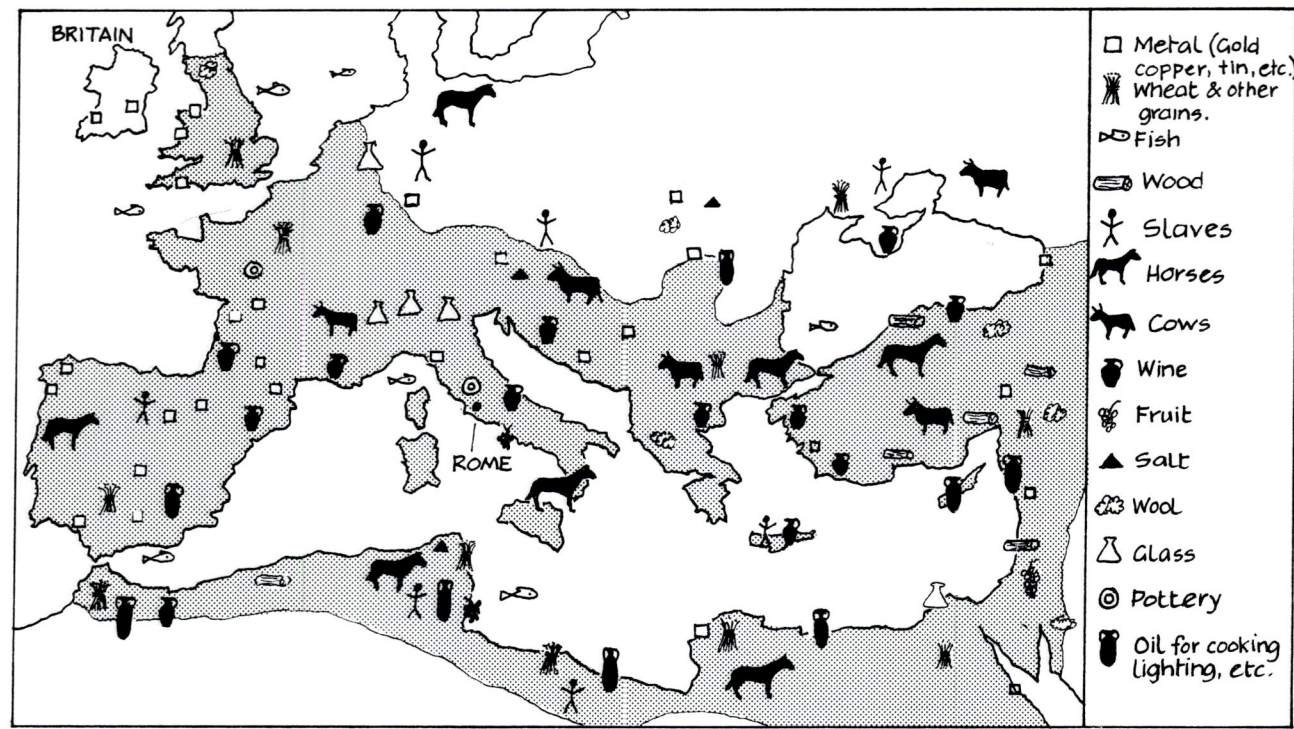

Some of the things traded in the Roman Empire.

A Roman carving of a ship carrying wine barrels.

A SOURCE

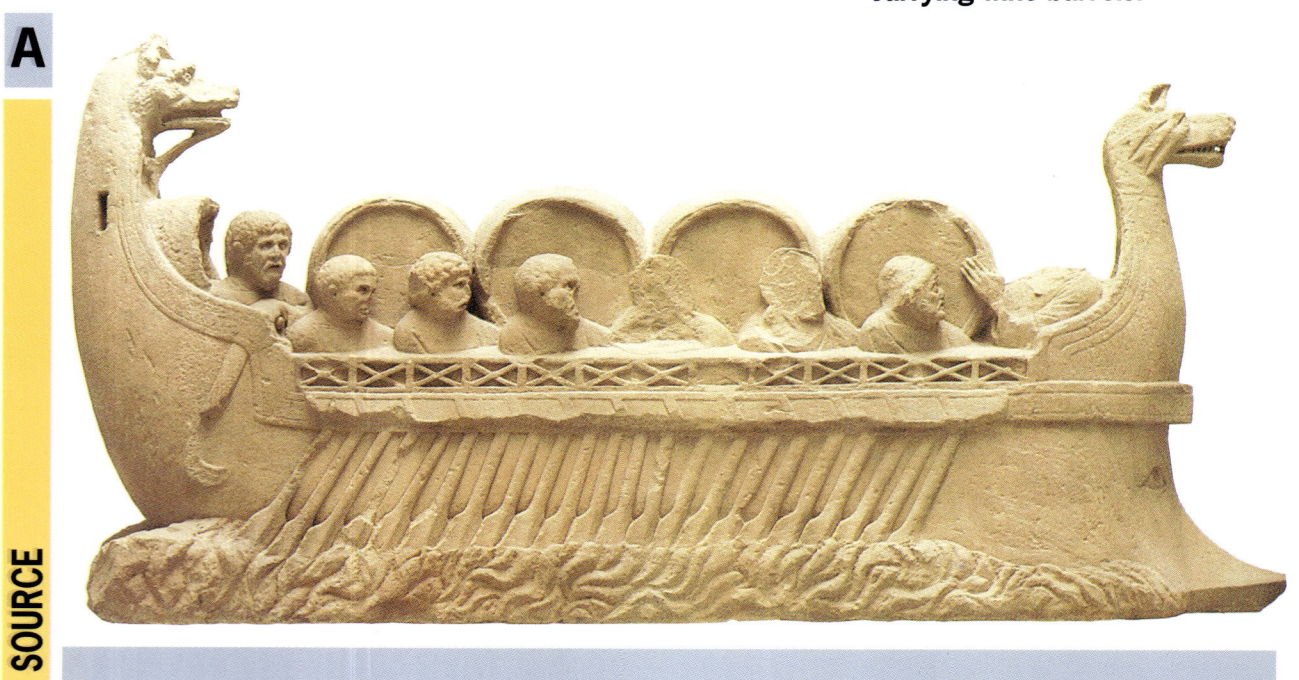

B SOURCE

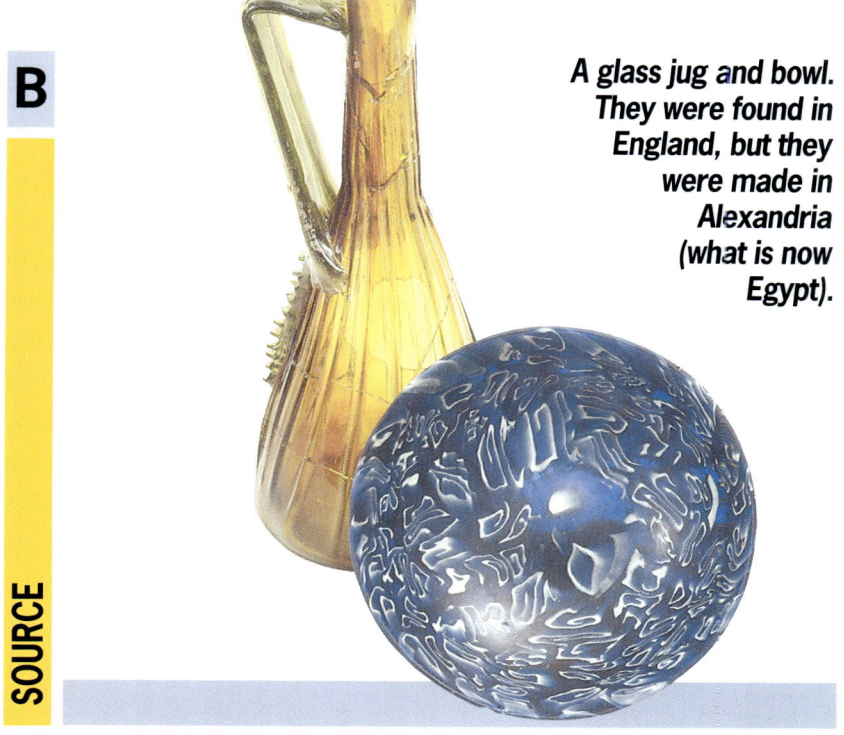

A glass jug and bowl. They were found in England, but they were made in Alexandria (what is now Egypt).

Local trade

Trade took place throughout the Empire. But some goods were also traded locally. For example, a farmer in Italy grew olives and picked them. He put them on a cart and drove them to the nearby town to sell them. With the money that he made he could buy something that he needed. Maybe he bought some meat at the butcher's shop.

C SOURCE

Storage jars for grain. They were buried to keep the grain cool. These jars were found in Ostia, the port that was closest to Rome.

Questions

Look at the map on page 36.
1 a Copy the goods from the list below that came from Britain.

   Horses   wine   slaves
   wheat and other grains
   metal   pottery

   b What sort of metals were there in the Roman Empire?
   c What was oil used for?
   d List some goods from outside the Roman Empire.

Think about:
Is there any evidence to show that the people of Rome bought or sold grain, wine and glass from other countries?

The sources and the map will help you to work this out.

THE ROMAN EMPIRE 37

3.6 Roman Towns and Cities

The Romans built many cities and towns all over the empire. If people in Britain wanted to build a town, they could send to Rome for a town plan like the one below.

Roman towns often needed walls to defend them.

A *Some Roman town walls still stand today. These are in what is now Turkey.*

SOURCE

38 THE ROMAN EMPIRE

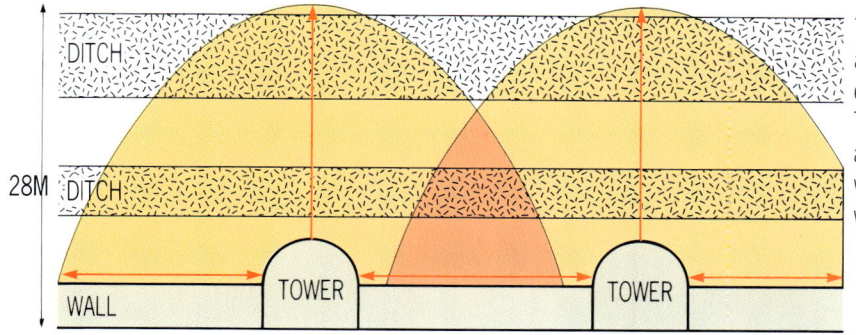

Town defences after the 4th century AD. Towers were added to the walls. Ditches were redug.

■ Area reached by weapons fired from the walls.

/// Area in front of walls, out of reach of defenders weapons.

→ Direction and distance weapons could be fired from town walls.

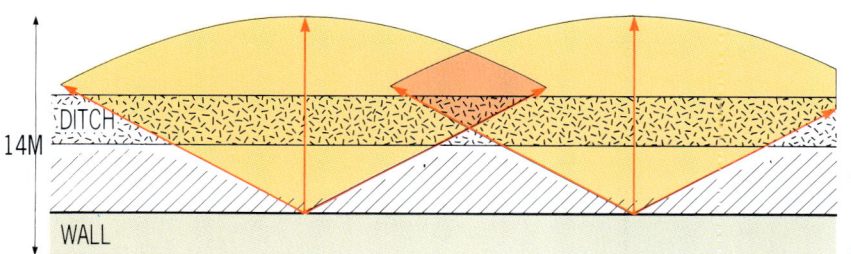

Town defences before the 4th century AD.

Towns and money

Lots of people lived in towns. They all earned money. They all needed food. So farmers brought chickens, eggs, pigs and so on to the towns to sell. The people who lived in the towns paid for the food in Roman coins. So more and more Roman coins were used and moved around the empire.

SOURCE B

A gold coin. People all paid taxes in Roman coins. Taxes were used in lots of ways. They were used to build everything from sewers to theatres. They were used to pay the army.

Questions

Look at the drawing of the town on page 38.

1 a What was the amphitheatre used for?
  b What was the forum?
  c How did water get to the public baths?
  d What was the basilica for?
  e How did many people get their drinking water?

Think about:
Look at the drawings on this page and at Source A. How can you tell that the town walls in Source A were built after the 4th century AD?

THE ROMAN EMPIRE 39

3.7 Buildings in Towns and Cities

A Roman carving of a shop.

Roman buildings

The Romans built houses, theatres, shops and temples. Many buildings were made from stone or brick. The stones or bricks were stuck together with concrete.

Roman concrete

The Romans invented concrete. They mixed cement, water, sand and bits of stone together. It made the buildings very strong.

This building was used for public games and races. The arches of the building carry all the weight, and because the building is in a circle all the arches support each other.

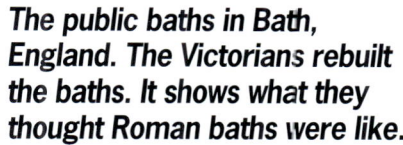

C

The public baths in Bath, England. The Victorians rebuilt the baths. It shows what they thought Roman baths were like.

Rich and poor

Rich people used marble to make their grand buildings beautiful. Poorer people made houses with wood and thatch or tiles.

D

A Roman carving of a shop.

Questions

Read **Roman buildings** and **Roman concrete**.

1 Copy the sentences below. Fill in the gaps.

The Romans built houses, temples, _____ and theatres in their towns and cities. Many buildings were made of brick or _____. The stones were stuck together with _____. This was made by mixing cement, bits of stone, water and _____. It made the buildings very _____.

> strong   shops   stone
> sand   concrete

Look at Sources A and D.

2 a What does the shop in Source A sell?
  b What does the shop in Source D sell?

3.8 Living in Towns and Cities

Public toilets in a Roman town in Africa. The Romans often built toilets like these directly over stone sewers, which carried the waste away at once. There were no sewers in the parts of the cities where the poor lived. These places were not as clean. This meant that more people became ill.

Rome in AD 1

By AD 1 there were over 1 million people living in Rome. This was a huge number for those days.

Rich and poor

Rich people lived in town houses. A town house was called a domus. The rooms were built around a courtyard. Poor people lived in blocks of flats. These were called insulae. They were badly built. They often burnt down.

An aqueduct in Africa. It took water 60 miles to the Roman city of Carthage.
It took 21 years to build.

C

A Roman mosaic from Africa. It shows gladiators fighting animals, and a prisoner being fed to a leopard.

Fire brigade

Emperor Augustus set up a fire service. There were 7,000 men in it. The firemen used handheld pumps.

Entertainment

Emperors put on big shows to keep the people happy. There were gladiator fights, chariot races and plays.

Questions

Read **Rich and poor**.
1 Copy the following sentences. Fill in the gaps.
   A rich person lived in a town house called a ____. Poor people lived in blocks of ____. These were called ____.

   flats   insulae   domus

Look at all the sources.
2 a How do historians know that some Roman cities had good supplies of water?
   b How do historians know that the Romans liked lots of entertainment?

D

A Roman theatre in Ephesus (in what is now Turkey).

3.9 Life in the Countryside

Farms

Most people in the Roman Empire lived in the countryside. They grew food and kept animals.

Rich Romans

Some Romans were very rich. They owned huge farms. Sometimes they owned farms in different places. A rich woman called Melania owned farms in Italy, Sicily, Africa, Spain and Britain. This was in the 4th century AD. She employed people to run her farms. They paid her rent.

All over the empire

The Roman Empire was enormous. In Britain it was cold and wet. Farmers kept cows and sheep and grew crops like oats and wheat. In North Africa it was hot. Farmers kept goats and grew crops like dates, grapes, figs and wheat.

B The plan of a Roman farmhouse did not change much over the years.

A modern archaeologist said this about farmhouses in the Middle East under all the years of Roman rule.

A modern reconstruction of a dining room in a rich Roman's farmhouse in about AD 350.

How they lived

Archaeologists have dug up many Roman country houses called villas. These were the homes of better-off farmers. Poorer people had wooden, thatched houses. These have not survived.

Farmers grew enough food to feed their families. If they had any spare food they sold it. A farmer who sold food could pay his taxes and buy pottery, brooches and tools. If archaeologists find things like this around farms, they know that a farmer was trading his food for other things.

C SOURCE

A Roman mosaic. It shows a house in North Africa.

D SOURCE

Many poorer farmers would have lived in houses like this in Roman Britain.

Questions

Read **Farms**.
1 Where did most people live in the Roman Empire?

Read **Rich Romans**.
2 Copy the sentences below. Choose one of the words in *italics* each time there is a choice.
Some rich Romans owned many *farms/fish*. In the 4th century AD/BC, a rich woman called *Mary/Melania* owned farms in many parts of the *Greek/Roman* Empire – Italy, Sicily, Britain, Africa and *the USA/Spain*. Other people ran the farms for her. They paid her *wages/rent*.

Read **How they lived**.
3 How do archaeologists know if a farmer was growing more than enough food to feed his family?

Look at Source A.
4 Would a room like this have been found in the farmhouses in Sources C and D? Explain your answer.

THE ROMAN EMPIRE 45

3.10 Roman Villas

What was a villa?

'Villa' is a Latin word. It means a house in the country or a farm. Most people think of a villa as a large Roman country house with a farm. Villas were fairly simple at first. Later, they were rebuilt in a more grand style. The farmworkers or slaves lived in one part of the villa. The owners lived in another part.

Everywhere the Romans went people copied their villas. There are Roman style villas from Britain to North Africa.

A Roman painting from about AD 150. It shows a farm in what is now Germany.

Hypocausts

The richest people had baths and underfloor heating. This underfloor heating was called a hypocaust. There were beautiful wall paintings and mosaics on the floor.

A Roman statue of a ploughman. It comes from what is now Germany.

A Roman mosaic from about AD 320. It shows a villa in North Africa.

Questions

1. **a** Copy the picture of the Roman hypocaust on this page. Mark the hot air with red arrows.
   b What sort of person do you think stoked the fire? Choose from the list below:

   a child   the owner   a slave

   a ploughman.

Look at Sources A and B.
2. **a** List the farm jobs you can see being done in the picture.
   b List the things that are different about the villas.

THE ROMAN EMPIRE   47

3.11 Religious Beliefs

Spirits

The Romans believed spirits protected their homes. One of these was Vesta. She was goddess of the hearth. Another one was Janus. He was god of the doorway.

Roman goddesses and gods

The Romans also worshipped many gods. Some of them are listed below:

Jupiter	chief god.
Juno	goddess of women and Jupiter's wife.
Venus	goddess of love.
Neptune	god of the sea.
Mars	god of war.
Minerva	goddess of wisdom and war.
Diana	goddess of hunting.
Apollo	god of the sun.
Ceres	goddess of harvest.

B SOURCE

It is my will that graves be undisturbed forever. If anyone disturbs them, I command that he be executed for grave robbery.

An order given by the emperor in the 1st century AD.

A SOURCE

A temple of the Roman god Jupiter. This temple is in North Africa.

C

A temple of the Persian god, Mithras. It was built underground in Rome.

Romans and other peoples' gods

The Romans were very easy-going about other peoples' gods. Often they just adopted new gods or goddesses wherever they went.

Christianity

This easy-going attitude seems to have changed when the Romans came in contact with Christianity. This was partly because they had to give up all the other gods to become Christian.

D

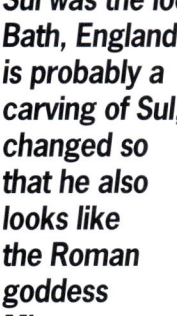

Sul was the local god in Bath, England. This is probably a carving of Sul, changed so that he also looks like the Roman goddess Minerva.

Questions

Look at the list of goddesses and gods on page 48.

1. Copy the list below. Match the Heads and Tails.

Mars	love
Apollo	chief god
Diana	sun
Jupiter	sea
Neptune	hunting
Ceres	war
Venus	harvest

Read Source B.

2. Copy the sentence below that says what Source B **proves**.
   People robbed graves.
   Everyone obeyed the emperor.
   Everyone respected graves.

3.12 The First Christians

Jesus Christ

Jesus Christ was a great teacher. He taught about living a good life, about believing in God and about life after death. Jesus was executed by the Romans in about AD 33. By this time there were many people who followed his teachings. They thought he was the son of their God. Jesus' followers were called Christians.

Christians and the Roman Empire

Christians said they could not worship all the Roman gods. They believed that they could only worship the Christian God. They believed worshipping lots of gods was wrong. This made some of the Roman emperors and people angry. Many Christians were killed.

B SOURCE

The Christians were torn apart by dogs and killed. Some were fixed to crosses, or burned to light up the night.

Written by Tacitus, a Roman, who lived from AD 56–115.

C SOURCE

The Christians swear not to steal, rob or commit adultery.

Written by Pliny, a Roman, who lived from AD 24–79.

A SOURCE

A British painting of Christians praying. It was painted in the 4th century AD.

D

A mosaic head of Jesus Christ from a Roman villa in Britain. It dates from the 4th century AD. The sign behind the head means 'Jesus Christ'.

The Roman emperor becomes a Christian

Gradually some Romans wanted to become Christians. The Emperor Constantine became a Christian in AD 324. After this more and more important people became Christians. Soon Christianity was the official religion of the Roman Empire.

E

Pieces of silver from Britain. They date from the 4th century AD.

Questions

Read **Jesus Christ**.
1 Write down the three things that Jesus taught about.

Read **Christians and the Roman Empire**.
2 What made the Roman emperors angry?

Read **The Roman emperor becomes a Christian**.
3 Which Roman emperor became a Christian in AD 324?

Look at all the sources.
4 a Which source tells you that Christians were not accepted in the Roman Empire in the 2nd century AD?
  b How do you know that Christianity had reached Britain by the 4th century AD?

THE ROMAN EMPIRE 51

4.1 The Empire in Crisis

The Roman Empire by AD 100

At first it seemed the Romans would conquer the world. They took Greece, Spain, Gaul and many other lands. By AD 100 the Roman empire was huge (see map on page 19).

AD 117 – the empire stops growing

Hadrian became emperor in AD 117. He saw the empire had grown as much as it could. Barbarians were all around the edges of the empire. To conquer more land would need a bigger army. This would cost a lot of money. Hadrian felt enough was enough. He built a wall in Britain, to keep out the northern tribes. It was called Hadrian's Wall. The Romans built forts and walls all around the empire.

Problems in the empire

The population in the Roman Empire fell. So there were fewer people to pay taxes, or join the army. We are not sure why the population fell. Maybe changes in the weather meant bad harvests and too little food. Maybe raids by tribes meant that farmers gave up growing food in some places. Maybe new diseases killed off many people.

Falling trade – 3rd century AD

In the 3rd century AD, tribes began to break through the forts and walls to raid the empire. It was dangerous to travel by road or ship. Traders did not want to travel. British people could not buy glass from Egypt.

B 5,000 a day are said to have died from the plague in Rome, and more in the country. It is possible that the plagues were smallpox and measles.

From 'Plagues and People', by W. McNeill, 1976. He was writing about illness AD 251–66.

A boat from Denmark. Danish pirates raided the Roman Empire in the 4th century AD. They may have used boats like this.

A

C SOURCE

A Roman fort, built in Britain in AD 275. It was one of many built to protect Britain against pirates.

Towns

There was less and less trade. So towns got smaller. Shops were left empty. Buildings fell down.

The Romans leave Dacia – AD 270

The barbarians in the east raided Dacia (see map on page 19) again and again. It was AD 270. The Roman army packed up and left Dacia. This was the beginning of the end of the Roman Empire.

D SOURCE

Pieces of Roman silver, found in Ireland. The Romans never conquered Ireland. They probably paid a pirate leader not to raid them.

Questions

Read **AD 117 – the empire stops growing**.

1 Copy the sentences below. Fill in the gaps.
Hadrian saw that the _____ had grown as much as it could. To conquer more _____ would need a bigger _____. Hadrian built a _____ in Britain. Hadrian's Wall was to keep out the northern _____. The Romans built other walls and _____. The Roman empire had stopped _____.

> army   growing
> empire   wall   land
> forts   tribes

Read **Problems in the empire**.

2 Draw three cartoon pictures to show three things that might explain the falling population in the empire.

THE ROMAN EMPIRE 53

4.2 The Collapse of the Empire

The army

By the 3rd century AD there were not enough soldiers to defend the Roman Empire. Soldiers were rushed to wherever there was trouble. Also emperors forced men to join the Roman army because there were not enough volunteers.

The edges of the empire

There were lots of barbarian tribes around the edges of the Roman Empire. Some emperors allowed these tribes to move into the empire as long as the men agreed to fight in the Roman army.

Splitting the empire – AD 285

The emperor decided he could not run the whole empire any longer. So he split it into two parts. There was an eastern empire and a western empire. This still didn't help matters. The population fell more and more. The people who were left had to pay more and more taxes. But still the tribes outside the empire attacked and attacked.

The fall of Rome – AD 410

The attacks got worse and worse. In AD 410, tribes of Goths attacked Rome. In AD 476, the last Roman emperor was overthrown. The western Roman Empire had collapsed. Only the eastern empire was left.

A

The Roman general Stilicho. He was a Vandal who fought for Rome.

B Should the Romans have trusted the defence of Rome to the gods?

Written by a Christian, who lived from AD 354–430.

C SOURCE

This mosaic shows of a Vandal who has captured a Roman villa in North Africa. It dates from AD 490.

Questions

Read **The army** and **The edges of the empire**.

1 Write a heading: **The 3rd century AD**. Copy the statements below that you think are true.

The Roman army was huge.
The Roman army was too small.
The army had to rush to wherever there was trouble.
Men were forced to join the army.
Men were stopped from joining the army.
Barbarians were allowed to move into the empire.
The tribes had to fight for Rome.

Look at the map.

2 How many different barbarian tribes attacked the Roman Empire?

The barbarian invaders of the Roman Empire in the 5th century AD.

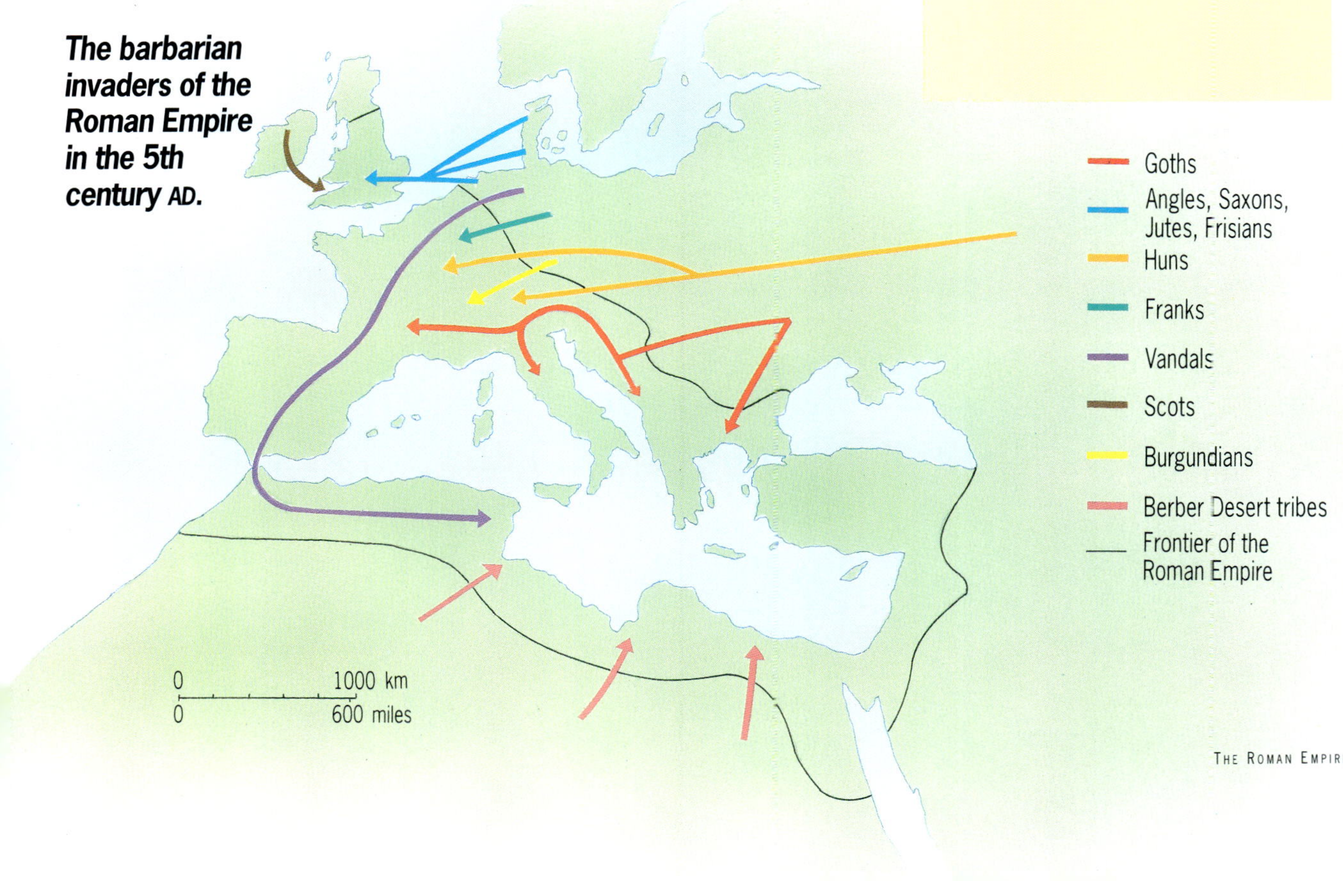

- Goths
- Angles, Saxons, Jutes, Frisians
- Huns
- Franks
- Vandals
- Scots
- Burgundians
- Berber Desert tribes
- Frontier of the Roman Empire

0   1000 km
0   600 miles

THE ROMAN EMPIRE 55

4.3 The Collapse of the Empire: Gaul

Roman Gaul

Gaul was made up of what is now France, Belgium and parts of Germany.

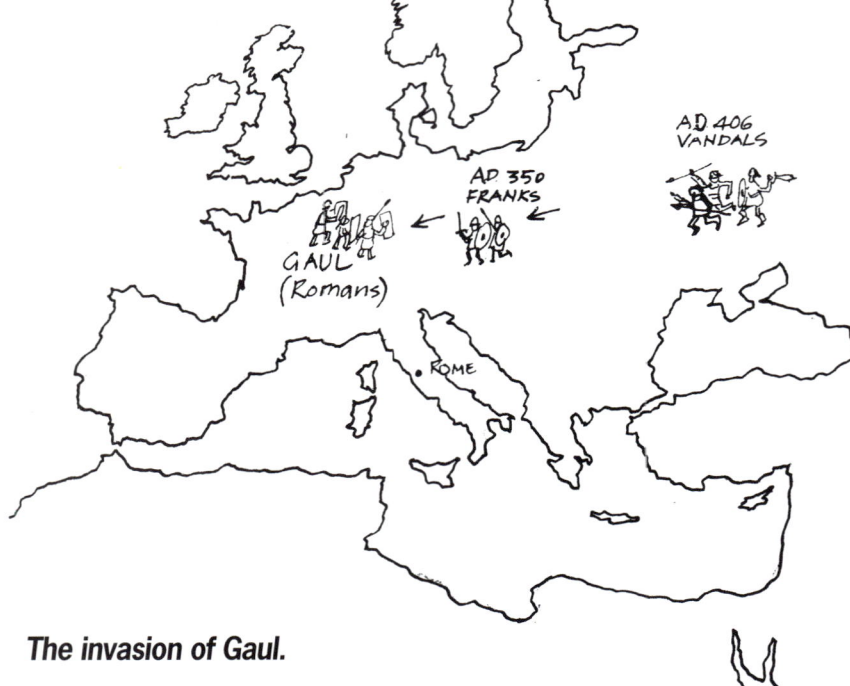

The invasion of Gaul.

The Franks

The Franks wanted to live like the Romans. Modern historians think that the Franks did not kill all the Romans in Gaul, or destroy all the farms. They wanted the farms themselves. Some Franks fought for the Romans against the Vandals. But gradually the Franks took over Gaul.

SOURCE A

Death, sorrow, destruction, fire.

From a poem about barbarians destroying Gaul. It was written in the 5th century AD.

SOURCE B

Roman villas still existed. They became the centres of villages.

From 'The Roman Villa', by J. Percival, 1976.

SOURCE C

Leontius (a Roman who lived in Gaul) owns three villas.

Written in about AD 550.

SOURCE D

Before the 5th century all the things that were buried with the dead were Roman things. During the 6th century Frankish things were buried in the graves.

From 'Blood of the British', by C. Hills, 1986.

E

Pieces of a sword found in the grave of a Frankish leader. The grave dates from about AD 482. The sword is decorated in a Roman style.

Questions

Look at the map on page 56.
1 a When did the Franks invade Gaul?
 b When did the Vandals invade Gaul?

Read Sources A, B and C.
2 Do Sources B and C agree or disagree with Source A? Explain your answer.

Look at Source E and read the caption.
3 What does this source tell you about what the Franks thought of Roman things?

4.4 The Collapse of the Empire: Britain

Coins and taxes – AD 410

The Romans lost Gaul. Then they lost Britain. The Roman army left. After AD 410, there were no more Romans to collect taxes. The Romans stopped sending coins to Britain too.

The end of trade

Ordinary people had no money to buy tools, pots, plates, knives and glasses. Farmers went back to just growing enough food for themselves and their families. They did not need to grow more food to sell so that they could pay their taxes. This was the end of the Roman system of buying and selling with money.

The end of the towns

Without taxes and trade there was no reason to have towns. People moved from the towns to the country, to grow food. No one lived in towns so the shops, houses and theatres fell down.

A

A Roman belt buckle. This one was worn by an Englishman buried in Essex in AD 400.

B Towns were destroyed. Survivors were killed or made into slaves forever.

A description of the Angles invading in AD 530, by a British monk who hated the English.

C
1 Cerdic and Cynric took the Isle of Wight and killed a few men.

2 Cerdic and Cynric took the Isle of Wight and killed many men.

Two versions of the victory of two English chiefs. An English monk re-wrote the book.

D We can imagine the Anglo-Saxon men storming camps, burning towns, and driving away the Roman Britons.

From 'History of England', by G.M. Trevelyan, 1926.

58 THE ROMAN EMPIRE

Angles and Saxons

When the Romans left, the Angles and Saxons moved in. They came from places like modern day Germany and Denmark. They settled in the part of Britain now called England (which means land of the Angles).

E **SOURCE**

The number of Anglo-Saxons who came to Britain was probably around tens of thousands. There were millions of Roman Britons.

From 'The Ending of Roman Britain', by A.E. Cleary, 1989.

F **SOURCE**

A pot made by a Roman British potter. The decoration on the pot is an Anglo-Saxon design.

G **SOURCE**

We cannot take it for granted that the Anglo-Saxons killed all the Roman Britons.

From 'Medieval Society and Economy', by M. Postan, 1978.

Questions

Read **Coins and taxes – AD 410**.

1 Copy the sentences below. Fill in the gaps.
   The Romans lost _____. Then they lost _____. After _____ there were no Roman _____ brought into Britain Also there were no Romans to collect _____ from the farmers and other people.

> coins   Britain   Gaul
> taxes   AD 410

Read all the sources.

2 Historians often disagree about what happened in the past.
   Which sources show you that two historians have disagreed about the way that the Anglo-Saxons behaved?

THE ROMAN EMPIRE

4.5 Survival in the East

Constantinople – capital of the eastern empire

It was AD 330. The Emperor Constantine built a new capital in Turkey. He named it after himself. The city of Constantinople became very famous. It is now Istanbul, in Turkey.

A mosaic showing Justinian's wife, Theodora, giving a gift to the Italian church.

Justinian and the eastern empire

The eastern empire was quite strong. In AD 554, the Emperor Justinian recaptured Rome. But not for long. The Roman Empire in the west had gone for good. But the eastern empire went on. There were Roman buildings in Constantinople and Roman laws were obeyed. This lasted for nearly a thousand more years.

B

SOURCE

The Church of St. Sophia, in Constantinople. Justinian had it built.

C The pressure from behind on the barbarian tribes was great, and besides, they could see great prizes ahead.

(Reasons for barbarian attacks on the Roman Empire.)

SOURCE

From 'History of the World', by J. Roberts, 1980.

Questions

Read **Constantinople – capital of the eastern empire**.
1 Where and when did Constantine build a new capital?

Look at Sources A and B.
2 What do they tell you about the eastern Roman empire? Choose three words from the list below.

poor   rich   skilled   small
modern   artistic   warlike

> **Think about:**
> Read Source C. Look at the map on page 55. Which tribe was pushing the other tribes from behind?

THE ROMAN EMPIRE **61**

4.6 The Importance of Rome

Spreading ideas

The Roman Empire was huge. The Romans made it safe for people to travel, so they did. They talked about new ideas, like Christianity. The ideas spread all over Europe. Roman things spread all over Europe too. Men sailed ships all around the coasts of the Roman Empire. It was possible to buy wine and grapes in places like Britain where it was too cold to grow them.

Today

There are still many signs of the Roman Empire today.

- The Latin language is used for many things, like the names of plants.

A

Italian fascists in the 1920s. Some are dressed like Romans. They wanted Italy to have a great empire again, like Rome.

B

A picture of a Roman scene, painted 1,300 years after Rome fell.

- Many of our words come from the Latin: video, navy, public, legal.
- There are many ruins of Roman buildings and roads all over Europe.
- Many of our roads today run along the same routes as Roman roads.
- Many laws in Europe are based on Roman laws.

D *A British coin. The letters 'D.G. Reg' are short for the Latin for 'By God's Grace: Queen'.*

C *A building in Oxford, England. It is built in the Roman style, but was not built until the 1700s.*

Questions

Read **Spreading ideas**.

1 Copy the sentences below. Fill in the gaps.
   The Roman Empire was very _____. The Roman army was strong, so it was safe for people to _____. Lots of people travelled and talked about new ideas like _____.

   | big   travel |
   | Christianity |

2 List as many things as you can that the Romans have left us today.

INDEX

Alexandria 37
Angles and Saxons 59
Apollo 48
aqueduct 42
Archaeologists 5, 31, 44, 45
arches 40
Armenia 26
Augustus 26, 27, 29, 43

barbarians 30, 31, 52, 53, 54, 55, 56, 61
Belgium 56
Bible, 28, 35
Britain 4, 5, 8, 24, 25, 35, 44, 45, 46, 51, 52, 53, 58, 62

Caesar 20, 21
Caligula 27,
Carthage 12,13, 42
centurion 14
chariot races 43
children 32, 33
Christian 27, 49, 50, 51
Christianity 49, 62
citizens 16, 17, 20, 21, 28, 29
Claudius 24, 25, 27,
Colchester 24, 25
concrete 40
Constantine 27, 60
Constaninople 60, 61
consuls 16

Dacia 53
Denmark 52, 59
domus 42

Egypt 26, 37, 52
Equites 28
Etruscans 10, 11

family 32, 45, 58
farms 44, 46
firemen 43
food 35, 39, 44, 45, 52
forum 17
France 56
Franks 56

Gauls 10, 20, 21, 52, 56, 58
Germany 35, 46, 47, 56, 59
gladiators 43
gods and goddesses 32, 48, 49, 54
God 50
Goths 54
Greece 52
Greeks 10, 29.

Hadrian 27, 29, 52
Hadrian's Wall 4, 5, 27, 52
Hannibal 12

heating 47
historians 4, 8, 56
hypocaust 47

insulae 42
Ireland 53
Italy 7, 10, 11, 12, 35, 37, 44, 62

Jesus Christ 50, 51
Justinian 60, 61

Kent 24

Latin 4, 35, 46, 62, 63
legion 14, 15
London 8, 9

marble 41
Marcus Aurelius 27
Mediterranean 34
Middle East 44
mosaics 35, 43, 45, 47, 51, 55, 60

Nero 27
North Africa 35, 42, 43, 44, 45, 46, 47, 48, 55

Ostia 37

parents 32
Patricians 28
Plebeians 28
public baths 41
public toilets 42

Republic 10, 11, 20, 26, 32
religion 48, 50, 51
roads 34, 35, 52, 63
Roman army 10, 14, 15, 16, 18, 20, 21, 25, 26, 28, 30, 31, 35, 39, 53, 54, 58
Roman coins 11, 13, 16, 18, 26, 30, 31, 35, 39, 58
Romulus 10, 11

Senate 16, 17, 26, 28
sewers 42
ships 34, 35, 36, 52, 62
shops 40, 41, 53
Sicily 12, 44
silver 7, 51, 53
slaves 29, 46
Spain 12, 20, 21, 44, 52

taxes 28, 35, 54
theatres 40, 43,58
towns 38, 39, 40, 42, 53, 58
town plans 38
trade 12, 13, 18, 36, 37, 45, 52, 53, 58

Trajan 27
Trajan's column 14
transport 34, 35
Turkey 38, 43, 60

Vandals 54, 55, 56
villas 45, 46, 51, 55
Virgil 4, 10, 18

wedding 32
wine 36
women 32